What people are

"Expectant is a much-needed scriptural refresher. The journey that Kylah took through God's Word is empowering. Many of the spiritual gems that He revealed to her were hidden treasures that I had yet to dig up in my own personal study. Yet, that is the beautiful thing about God. He has placed countless gems in His Word for us to discover. My soul is so grateful that I had the opportunity to take a deep dive into this devotional. It is a blessing and a must read!"

SaMonna Watts, Esq., *Speaker, Trainer, Author and Coach*

"God longs to have a relationship with us, and throughout our lives, He finds creative ways to capture our attention. Kylah Martin's debut book, *Expectant,* will take you on an adventure to activate your faith, one verse at a time, through every book of the Bible. Joining Kylah on this adventure is an experience of prayer and an expansion of faith with an authentic and compassionate person by your side.

"You'll be drawn in by Kylah's passionate invitation to go deeper with God through His Word. If you've always wanted to dig deep into the Bible, but were unsure where to start,

Kylah Martin's *Expectant* provides the perfect opportunity."

Rachel Lemons Aitken, author of *Fish Food* and founder of the *Digital Discipleship* ministry, South Pacific Division

"Expectant is the devotional that we need for such a time as this. In it, Kylah takes the reader on a journey through familiar scripture passages and unearths gems in those books of the Bible not often read. Her ability to challenge, yet encourage while sharing personal reflections is a gift, and as the reader you will be the deserving recipient of it. Thank you, Kylah, for reminding us to remain expectant before God, stay expectant of what He can do for and through us, and be expectant of who He reveals Himself to be to us, each day…if we expect it."

Kimberley D. Caines-Best, *Speaker and Bible Teacher*

"Kylah will inspire and encourage you to see God in unexpected places as she shares her heart and journey in experiencing God, a God who loves you and wants to bless you more here and now."

Joanne Cortes, *Pastor*

"Expectant, by Kylah Martin, is the devotional we need right now. Reading the captivating stories coupled with the profound spiritual insights she shares in this book will encourage and challenge you towards spiritual growth."

Claudia M. Allen, *Online Content Manager for Message Magazine*

Expectant

Expectant

What if there was a gift
in every book of the Bible
just for you?

Kylah R.S. Martin

Cover photo/Unsplash.com

Cover photo edited by Jahni M. A. Smith

Author photo by Gianna Snell Photography

Layout design by Seek and Save Design

Scripture quotations taken from The Holy Bible, New International Version®, NIV®

Copyright © 1973, 1978, 1984, 2011 by Biblica, Inc.™

Used by permission. All rights reserved worldwide.

ISBN 978-1-7363173-0-3

Dedication

To Mrs. Edith VanLowe.

For planting a seed of possibility in the heart of this child. Thank you.

In Loving Memory

Daddy,

Otero F. W. Allers

In my heart forever. And ever.

Aunt Kim,

Kim M. J. Hendrickson

The book dedication was also meant to read this way:

> For your unceasing devotion to God which has inspired
> me from childhood until today. Thank you.

We'll talk about it one sweet day.

"Open my eyes that I may see wonderful things in Your law."

Psalm 119:18

"... You did awesome things that we did not expect ..."

Isaiah 64:3

Contents

Introduction

More Than Expected

It all began one "September to Remember." My pastor (also my husband; I love that guy!) issued a challenge to our church. For the month of September, we were invited to read one chapter of Proverbs a day, two on the last day. This wasn't anything too daunting. Honestly, it was a challenge I had personally taken on before.

The plot twist was this. Each day, with each chapter, we were challenged to learn at least one verse. Every day. Not one for the week. One for each day. I was fleetingly both critical and skeptical of the challenge.

Every day?

Surely it was the enemy planting that seed of doubt. I

should have been immediately energized and ready to jump right in because committing scripture to memory has been a goal on every list of mine. And full disclosure, that goal has consistently been met with less than stellar results.

Shaking off the doubt, my competitive juices began to swirl. "This is a challenge?" I mused. "For everyone? I will have the accountability of community (*clearly needed*), the opportunity to motivate others (*happy to*), and a chance to *win*?" Well, why not!

September neared, and my excitement grew. As God would have it, the day before the challenge began, a guest speaker visited our church. In his sermon, he referenced the common belief that it takes 21 days to form a habit. He said that is actually inaccurate. It takes a 21-day effort three times over. In other words, forming a habit takes 63 days.

Hmmm! I was intrigued. In that moment I was convinced that September wouldn't be the end of my endeavor to memorize scripture. I *had* to keep it going. Within the space of a few minutes, there in the middle of the sermon, it settled nicely into my heart just how. Borrowing from our current challenge to learn a Proverb a day, at the end of the month I would roll on to learn a verse a day, one from each book of the Bible. 63 days to form a habit. 66 books. 63 + a bonus three? Absolutely!

So, I settled into the challenge, taking it to heart. The month progressed, and I was loving it! It was indeed a September to remember. The whole experience was wonderful. Rolling into October, I began selecting and learning verses from a different book daily (in no set order). I saved them to a note on my phone. I reviewed them often and did my best to keep up. And I did it! I selected and learned a verse a day from a book a day.

As I neared the end, I was at a loss for what to do next. Have you ever had that uneasy sense when a particular devotional experience is nearing its end? Well, as it turned out, God had more in those very verses for me. I felt impressed that it wasn't time to completely move on from that experience just yet. Each verse resonated with me in some way, and I needed more time with them.

That is how we arrived here. This is a window into my devotional experience – my two rounds of "63 + 3" as it were, all rolled into one. It was pure joy to first learn the verses and then circle back to reflect on and capture how each spoke to my heart, making it even more personal.

I'm so glad you've decided to join me. I pray that what has blessed me so much will overflow to you. I hope that something about what you read and experience in these pages will nurture a place in your heart that compels you toward a dynamic, growing relationship with God. With every reading, I've left some space for you to jot down what has spoken to your heart. It can come from the reading or it can come from another verse that is lodged in your heart from the book of the Bible that is referenced.

Beyond this, here's my invitation, my *challenge*: try the 63 + 3 *Expectant* journey for yourself. Find a verse in every book of God's Word. Some books will be replete with verses jumping off the page (*how will I choose?*). Others will be obscure (*what will I choose?*). It might be tough, but it will be worth it. Capture what each says to you and why it's meaningful. You can flesh out your thoughts as you select your verses, or you can go through and return at the end of that initial experience to reflect like I did. You can do this alone, or you can do this with friends. There are no real rules. I simply offer these suggestions as a way to navigate the terrain of God's Word, hiding it in your heart while enjoying the view.

I truly believe that, for you, an unrivaled experience with God awaits when you come to meet Him every day, heart wide open. Never disappointed. Always expectant.

1

Uproot It!

Luke 17:6, *"He replied, 'If you have faith as small as a mustard seed, you can say to this mulberry tree, 'Be uprooted and planted in the sea,' and it will obey you.'"*

Any time I've encountered this text, I have always wanted to better understand it, to truly grasp and to fully experience it. It sounds like a kind of sanctified superpower. Wouldn't you agree?

In search of greater clarity this time, I literally found myself all around the mulberry tree. Here I was, looking online for anything of intrigue about mulberry trees. Maybe an intricate root system or fruity limbs would reveal something of practical interest. I found nothing.

The next morning, I could not leave this text completely. I took my time and read the surrounding verses, and there it was, unexpected, but noteworthy.

The verses leading up to Luke 17:6 articulate Jesus' words to the disciples. He challenged them on forgiveness and living uprightly in such a way that they would not cause people to stumble. It is in response to *this* that the apostles exclaim, "Increase our faith!" Jesus replies to their exasperation, "If you have faith as small as a mustard seed, you can say to this mulberry tree, 'Be uprooted and planted in the sea,' and it will obey you."

There are matters of the heart, planted as firm as a tree, that need to be uprooted. Perhaps the symbolic uprooting of this tree pertains to the power of faith to uproot unforgiveness, unhealthy habits, or poor choices that seem immovable. Jesus says, "Don't despair! Have faith! Live by faith! Speak in faith!" By our faith, moreover *by our words backed by faith*, we can expect the landscape of our hearts and lives to be transformed to the glory of God.

Lord, thank You for the gems in Your Word. I pray for the boldness, commitment, and determination to experience a transformed "heart-scape." You said it is possible! Empower me with confidence to speak faith-filled, transformative words. I want to behold with my eyes and experience in my heart the radical working of that faith. Please grow every ounce of faith that I have, but please help me never to forget the power of even a small measure. Thank You for keeping me through this faith journey thus far. You are amazing to me. Amen.

Just for me in *Luke*

2

Reframe Your Thinking

2 Corinthians 12:9-10, "*But He said to me, 'My grace is sufficient for you, for My power is made perfect in weakness.' Therefore, I will boast all the more gladly about my weaknesses, so that Christ's power may rest on me. That is why, for Christ's sake, I delight in weaknesses, in insults, in hardships, in persecutions, in difficulties. For when I am weak, then I am strong.*"

Rarely, and certainly not instinctively, do we attach "delight" to difficulty. If we in any way feel weak, insulted, or persecuted, these feelings are not accompanied with a chest swell of pride and boastful anticipation. The truth is, we do not relish the idea of being stuck in, or even temporarily encountering, hardships.

But, if we avail of the generous gift of God's grace, then our weaknesses are outdone by His power. And oddly, despite our weakness, we appear strong. What Christ's power resting on us looks like may vary every time, but perhaps that's where the delight comes in. When we give the problem to God and speak confidently (*boast*) in the face of the trial, we can grab the popcorn because God is about to do something that we could not.

In my life, Lord, be glorified! Please help me to reframe my thinking and to put all my trust, my hopeful, boastful expectation, in You. Thank You for Your power. Thank You for the generous gift of Your grace through which You impart that power to us in our frailty. You are more than wonderful and You alone make this journey called life worth living. I love You. Amen.

Just for me in 2 Corinthians

3

Never Outdone

Job 42:2, *"I know that You can do all things; no purpose of Yours can be thwarted."*

God has no limits. There are no boundaries that can contain or restrain Him. He is boundless! He can do all things and no situation, condition, or plan of the enemy threatens that.

This is the confidence we need to carry with us every single day. Any limiting belief we have about ourselves must crumble in the shadow of this bigger-than-all-our-problems truth: none of God's purposes or plans for us can be thwarted.

In all things and through all things, God can do anything!

God, I am amazed when I pause to consider Your immeasurable greatness – a power that can never be outdone. Your purposes will always prevail. I trust You with my life. I will take courage every day in the confidence that You can do all things. I am in perfect hands when I am in You! Amen.

Just for me in *Job*

4

Tears to Joy

Psalm 126:5, "Those who sow with tears will reap with songs of joy."

I love the notion of joy. A deep, visceral, gut level state of peace, happiness, well-being, contentment, and satisfaction all rolled into one. It's my preferred state of being. In fact, it's what I aim to inspire in others. Joy.

Life's reality, however, says this: sometimes tears precede joy. Sometimes hurt, sadness, and confusion creep in and attempt to sabotage joy. Rather than allowing this to manifest as a crippling reality, know this: our pain does not have to be fruitless. Sow with those tears. Continue to invest in what would be productive. With the strength that God provides, pursue what would be for the greater good. In due time we will reap a harvest of joy. Don't give up!

Lord, it is not always the easiest to position my mind this way. Pushing through pain, giving of myself, investing my energy, heart, and soul in what would be for good despite hurt, sadness, and despondency is hard, but that is part of the journey to, or back to, joy. Please help me keep my eyes on You knowing that You can and will transition my tears to joy. Amen.

Just for me in **Psalms**

5

What's Wise, Guys?

James 3:17-18, *"But the wisdom that comes from heaven is first of all pure; then peace-loving, considerate, submissive, full of mercy and good fruit, impartial and sincere. Peacemakers who sow in peace reap a harvest of righteousness."*

James 1:5 tells us that if we lack wisdom, we should ask God for it. He will give it to us. Generously! What exactly does that look like? How do we know if we're operating with wisdom, specifically, God-given wisdom? James 3 distinguishes heavenly wisdom from worldly wisdom.

Heavenly wisdom is "first of all pure." There is no corruption or deceit in God's genre of wisdom. It is untainted. It is "peace-loving;" therefore, the default response of the wise person is to find equilibrium. This disposition is beneficial for a righteous life, character, and reward (v. 18). It is "considerate." It is disposed to considering all factors at hand without premature judgment. It is "submissive." At times wisdom says, "Not me. I must step aside and allow the powers that be, to be." It is "full of mercy." The response of the wise is bathed with compassion.

Wisdom from above is also full of "good fruit." Godly wisdom produces favorable outcomes. Good root, good fruit! Further, wisdom from God is saturated with the fruit of the Spirit – love, joy, peace, patience, kindness, goodness, faithfulness, gentleness, and self-control (Galatians 5:22-23). It is "impartial." This tells us that there is consistent application of wisdom, complete with all that heaven packages in it. Finally, it is "sincere." It is not contrived. It comes from an authentic place that only God can create in us. This is why we *must* ask God for it.

James also details what earthly, unspiritual, and demonic wisdom looks like (James 3:14-16). Rather than being possessed by "envy and selfish ambition" (James 3:14), the "wise and understanding" will "show it by their good life" (James 3:13). Let's strive to embody heavenly wisdom, leaving no room for the worldly counterfeit.

God, I am asking for the liberal gift of wisdom that comes from heaven. It is exciting to me that this gift is transformative in this life and fits me for eternal life with You. Amen.

Just for me in *James*

6

I'm Spent

Proverbs 4:7, "*The beginning of wisdom is this: Get wisdom. Though it cost all you have, get understanding.*"

Do not subscribe to the notion that wisdom is unattainable. For every wise person, wisdom had a beginning. If you don't have it, you can get it. Period. Ask of God – He will grant it liberally. So says James 1:5.

Now that we've cleared that up, let's address the elephant in the room. If wisdom is free, what is the deal with understanding? Why exactly does it cost "all you have?" Why so pricey?

Maybe it is simply this: understanding requires a lifetime

of sacrificial investment. It involves regularly and permanently releasing the idea that my version is the only version and leaves nothing more to be understood. This looks like trusting self less and acknowledging the limitations of my singular perspective. Obtaining understanding often encompasses listening patiently, factoring in another vantage point, reframing a neatly packaged belief, processing and filtering, exercising patience, and exuding empathy.

Do you see the price tag racking up?

All of this does not necessarily demand a shift in belief. Rather, it's the currency that affords greater awareness, greater relatability, greater understanding.

No questions about it, understanding *is* pricey. It's an ongoing investment, and according to this Word, no matter the price tag, it is worth it.

God, I thank You for the gift of wisdom that is available upon a sincere ask. You tell us that the price of understanding is worth the expense. I pray that my mind will be opened and postured towards understanding, whatever the cost. May I grow in empathy for others, find common ground with others, and always magnify You to others as fruit of expending myself for the sake of understanding. Amen.

Just for me in *Proverbs*

7

You've Got My Full Attention

Daniel 6:13, *"Then they said to the king, 'Daniel, who is one of the exiles from Judah, pays no attention to you, Your Majesty, or to the decree you put in writing. He still prays three times a day.'"*

Indulge me as I start on a note unrelated to the verse of the day. It just impressed me so much. In Daniel 3, the "three Hebrew boys" were not mentioned by name until verse 12. Their story of fearless allegiance, braving flames rather than cowering before an idolatrous image, could easily *not* have been about them. They could have remained among the anonymous "satraps, prefects, governors, advisers, treasurers, judges, magistrates, and other provincial officials." Yet, their undaunted stand and their few words cemented them in

Biblical history as permanent witnesses to the power of our God. I love that!

What took me back to Daniel 3 in the first place was this simple, yet profound, phrase appearing in our key text, Daniel 6:13, "Daniel . . . pays no attention to you, Your Majesty." How familiar! In Daniel 3:12 the *exact* indictment had been given of Shadrach, Meshach, and Abednego.

Despite nationwide decrees and personal threats, these four men exhibited a rare genre of faithfulness and undivided commitment to God. Their God-centered allegiance surpassed political correctness, the risk of offending, or any care about public scrutiny. None of that mattered. Their attention and true devotion were due to the King of the Universe. His instructions and decrees were primary. Without exception, *He* had their full attention.

God, I owe You alone my full attention. Help me to keep my eyes singularly on You, no matter what system or person of "power" demands otherwise. You are the only wise God. You are caring, loving, powerful, and mighty to save. I trust You entirely. Amen.

Just *for me in* **Daniel**

8

Damage Control

Hosea 6:1, *"Come let us return to the Lord. He has torn us to pieces, but He will heal us; He has injured us, but He will bind up our wounds."*

God's sovereignty can be baffling. He makes tough calls, and as a result, we experience tough seasons, sometimes for reasons we won't even know or understand. For many people, this is off-putting. "You want me to serve a God like *this*?" I envision a sea of such hurt, devastated, confused people with their backs turned toward God.

Then comes Hosea 6:1. A call for the Israelites to return to the Lord. A call to give Him another chance to be their God – *our* God! And He offers such a profound yet paradoxical reason – He brought us to this season of hurt, but He is capable to (and He will) fix it. He cares for us. He won't leave us broken. He knows exactly what needs mending and He is the only one who can do so 100% of the time. He has damage control in His plan.

Therefore, the best place for us to be in our pain and brokenness is not with our backs to God, but in His loving arms. He will heal us. He will bind up our wounds.

Lord, thank You for Your loving care and Your ability to bring us through painful and difficult seasons. So many people nurse resentment toward You, unable to reconcile the pain You permit. Sadly, they fail to see that it is a paralyzing existence to stay there without allowing You – trusting You – to bind up their wounds. I pray that we will always bear in mind Your compassion and that You always have our very best at heart. Help us to trust You to come through on the other side of the coin. Heal us. Bind up our wounds, and please, save us at last. Amen.

Just for me in *Hosea*

9

Advance Planning with My Name on It

Ephesians 2:10, *"For we are God's handiwork, created in Christ Jesus to do good works, which God prepared in advance for us to do."*

What a thought! We are the careful, intentional work of God's hand and a part of His plan. This is such a profound reminder that fills me with hope, anticipation, expectation, and motivation. God has crafted us for a specific purpose: to do good works. His careful attention ensured that we entered the world on time to meet up with what, in advance, He prepared for us to do. That means, we can and should live in anticipation of doing something every day that makes God smile and say, "That's good."

From the very beginning of time, this has been God's pattern with mankind (Genesis 1:26). In this single verse, possibly a single breath, God announces what He will do (make mankind), how He will do it (in His image), and with what purpose (to rule and to be fruitful). He created and blessed mankind with clarity on the good work that was prepared in advance for them to do. Genesis 1:26-31 is worth reading just to be reminded of God's intentionality with us from the beginning.

That reminder is encouraging and should compel us to seek God daily, asking Him to show us the paths He has for us. We must keep it in heart and mind that God considers us His handiwork. We are one of a kind, designed for a good work that God intentionally placed us here to do. We were not an afterthought, nor was the work He had in mind for us. So, we have every reason to live expectantly, with anticipation and readiness on life's journey, knowing that God has us in His plan.

Open my eyes and sensitize my heart, Lord. I am willing and ready to follow Your lead every day of my life. Amen.

Just for me in *Ephesians*

10

Finding God

Jeremiah 29:13, *"You will seek Me and find Me when you seek Me with all your heart."*

God wants to be found by us. What's more, He tells us just how to do so. "Seek Me with all your heart," He says, "and you *will* find Me."

You *will*. I like that. It is a clear, definitive guarantee that a wholehearted pursuit of God *will* result in finding God and connecting with Him. I want this guarantee to be my reality and yours too.

God, I commit all of my passion to seeking Your heart and finding You in every day and in every situation. I'm so thankful that there is no secret, prohibitive process involved. My sincere prayer is that nothing will ever take away from my wholehearted pursuit of You. This I pray in Your matchless name, Amen.

Just for me in *Jeremiah*

11

Living My Blessed Life!

Deuteronomy 28:8, "*The Lord will send a blessing on your barns and on everything you put your hand to. The Lord your God will bless you in the land He is giving you.*"

This is a big promise, and God is a big God who is more than capable of fulfilling this promise. God has prosperity in mind for you and for me. He has abundant life in store. He has plans for us that He wants to flourish. When we follow Him, He will bless *everything* we put our hands to. He will give us a blessing, and then He will turn around and bless us *in* our blessing! What a good, good, generous God we serve!

Lord, I want every blessing You have in mind for me to be mine! Please don't allow me to get in Your way. Keep me true to Your call, obedient to Your Word, and dedicated to nurturing a loving relationship with You. Amen.

Just for me in *Deuteronomy*

12

Well-Equipped by God to Please God

Hebrews 13:20-21, "*Now may the God of peace, who through the blood of the eternal covenant brought back from the dead our Lord Jesus, that great Shepherd of the sheep, equip you with everything good for doing His will, and may He work in us what is pleasing to Him, through Jesus Christ, to whom be glory for ever and ever. Amen.*"

God, my God, *your* God, is a God of great peace, great power, and great care. He equips us for *everything* He calls us to. In choosing to follow through on what He calls and equips us to do, He enables us to please Him *and* to glorify Him! How low-pressure and mind-blowing is *that*? *He* does it!

Yet, from time to time, we get sidetracked by our own

deficiencies. We allow the lies of the enemy to divert our attention from "the God of peace" to our frailties. This quote says it well:

> Many who are really conscientious and who desire to live for God, [the enemy] too often leads to dwell on their own faults and weaknesses, and thus by separating them from Christ he hopes to gain the victory. . . . Commit the keeping of your soul to God, and trust in Him. . . . Put away all doubt; dismiss your fears. Say with the apostle Paul, "I live, yet not I, but Christ liveth in me." . . . If you will leave yourself in His hands, He will bring you off more than conqueror through Him that has loved you.[1]

When we get caught up on the limitations of our own ability, we must remember this very truth. *He* equips us. *He* works in us. *He* doesn't fail.

Lord, keep my eyes on You. I need not focus on myself, nor the capabilities that I can see in myself. All of my confidence can rest squarely and securely in You. I must constantly behold You. This theme is reoccurring. How good You are God! Amen.

Just for me in *Hebrews*

13

Faithful, Intentional, Personal

Joel 2:23, "'*Be glad, people of Zion, rejoice in the Lord your God, for He has given you the autumn rains because He is faithful. He sends you abundant showers, both autumn and spring rains, as before.*'"

All around us there is evidence of God's faithfulness. Have you noticed? It's a great reason to be glad and rejoice. The rain doesn't just fall; He sends it. Seasons come and go as He ordains. God is in control. He is dependable. He is faithful.

This is not just evident in the natural realm, but also in the personal. Joel 2:23 doesn't say "He has given rain" or "He sends showers," though those are facts. He actually makes it personal – He has given *you* the autumn rains; He sends *you* abundant showers. And He does this because He is faithful to *you*!

Did you *feel* that? Did your heart just skip a beat like mine did? God is faithful to *you*. He intentionally orchestrates blessings to shower *your* path. He supplies *your* most essential needs. He gives *you* reasons to rejoice. Even when you navigate life's challenges, rehearse the amazing things God has done before. He is unlimited in His capacity to do "amazing" again. Rejoice! Fully embrace the personal interest God has in *you*.

Thank You, Lord, for evidence of Your great faithfulness. Thank You for this amazing reason to be glad and rejoice. You indeed are good, and what You do is good! Amen.

Just for me in Joel

14

Living Life Mentored

John 8:31-32, "To the Jews who had believed Him, Jesus said, 'If you hold to My teaching, you are really My disciples. Then you will know the truth, and the truth will set you free.'"

Hear ye! Hear ye!

This is a PSA to every believer: Cling to the words and teachings of Jesus, and be free!

There is a sense of rest, peace, and assurance when we are under the direct tutelage of someone who has mastered whatever it is that we are undertaking. Like a business coach to a new entrepreneur, a sports coach to the aspiring triathlete, a veteran teacher to the first-year newbie, the voice of each makes such a difference in the confidence of the student.

The student becomes aware of new and better approaches to the craft, and only on the strength of advice received, is willing to try them.

So, why not learn from the Master? What great confidence we can have by holding to His teachings and doing just what He says. That's freedom. That's a life of peace, leaning *not* on our own understanding (Proverbs 3:5), but resting on the lessons from the Master Teacher.

Lord, please help me to trust You always as the Master of all things. Self-reliance is so limiting, but it battles for preeminence. I want to experience the freedom and abundant life that tuning in to Your voice and following Your word provides. I'm excited about the life of freedom I will find in trusting You more! Amen.

Just for me in *John*

15

My Desires: Consecrated or Corrupted?

Jude 1:18-23, *"They said to you, 'In the last times there will be scoffers who will follow their own ungodly desires.' These are the people who divide you, who follow mere natural instincts and do not have the Spirit. But you, dear friends, by building yourselves up in your most holy faith and praying in the Holy Spirit, keep yourselves in God's love as you wait for the mercy of our Lord Jesus Christ to bring you to eternal life. Be merciful to those who doubt; save others by snatching them from the fire; to others show mercy, mixed with fear—hating even the clothing stained by corrupted flesh."*

A re your instincts consecrated? Psalm 37:4 admonishes, "Take delight in the Lord and He will give you the desires of your heart." This differs severely from our "mere natural instincts" which, unguided by the Holy Spirit, are based on ungodly and corrupted desires. Praise the Lord, God is bigger than our carnal desires. He can transform our hearts as we "delight" in Him – that is, as we grow in our faith, commune with Him in prayer, and experience and express His love.

The opportunity to put God's love on display is made clear in this text. Though the early part of Jude 1:18-23 warns against "scoffers," the end reveals the heart posture we should maintain toward such people. We should see them through the lens and love of God. We might assume that this love is to be expressed uniformly. After all, a scoffer's a scoffer! Right? However, here we learn differently.

There are some scoffers who are in a valley of doubt. Show them mercy. Be compassionate and kind and patient toward them. There are those who need immediate rescue. Snatch them "from the fire." Still there are others who should experience mercy, even while we maintain a healthy emotional distance. That's "mercy, mixed with fear."

The Lord will give the wisdom to navigate such interactions. Our primary commitment must be to grow in Him, to commune with Him, and to abide in His love so that our desires will be transformed from corrupt to consecrated. Then we can live and wait in peace for Him to bring us to eternal life.

Lord, thank You for the blessing of consecrated desires. Thank You for the leadership You thus provide in my interactions with others. Please help me to grow in my "most holy faith," to pray always in the Spirit, and to abide in Your love. I cling to Psalm 37:4, and I relish the truth that this can be my consistent reality. I trust You with my heart. Consecrate all of it I pray, in Jesus' name, Amen.

Just for me in *Jude*

16

You Don't Have to Work So Hard!

Matthew 11:28-30, *"Come to Me, all you who are weary and burdened, and I will give you rest. Take My yoke upon you and learn from Me, for I am gentle and humble in heart, and you will find rest for your souls. For My yoke is easy and My burden is light."*

In humility, know that it's not all about you. You do not have to prove yourself or take on unnecessary cares to validate yourself. You don't have to work so hard!

We all have a load to bear, and carrying a load is exhausting! But as we partner with Jesus, we learn new ways to muscle up: gentleness, humility, and dependence on Him.

He *will* give us rest. That is the sure result of coming to

Him and connecting with Him. Rest equals relief. Rest equals freedom from care. Rest equals peace of heart and mind. Rest equals ease.

Come to Jesus and let Him be your example and partner in this life. Abandon the thought that you must prove your strength and bear every load alone. As you continue to move forward with life's inevitable burdens, accept the rest that He offers. Trust Him to ease your load and lighten your burden. He can. He will.

Yes please, Lord! I don't know why sometimes doing the "hard" work is most celebrated, but I am ready to make easy gains with You. Help me to surrender and to connect with You every day. Thank You for the promise of rest. Thank You for a fresh reminder (that I will likely need again and again) that I don't have to work so hard. Amen.

Just for me in *Matthew*

17

Behind the Scenes

2 Kings 6:16-17, *"'Don't be afraid,' the prophet answered. 'Those who are with us are more than those who are with them.' And Elisha prayed, 'Open his eyes, Lord, so that he may see.' Then the Lord opened the servant's eyes, and he looked and saw the hills full of horses and chariots of fire all around Elisha."*

God is at work in ways that we cannot see, so we need to borrow Elisha's response and tell ourselves: "Don't be afraid!" "Don't worry!" "Don't be stressed!" "Don't focus on what you see!" God is ahead of the game, already positioned to meet us at the scene of every trial. What God can and will do is far beyond anything we could orchestrate to meet our own needs.

In this story, God revealed in a brilliant display how He was working literally behind the scenes on behalf of Elisha (and by extension his servant). Sometimes God reveals to us what He's doing and how He's working. Sometimes He doesn't. The fact remains, He has endless, unimaginable ways to meet our needs. He is dependable and capable. He is trustworthy. We must remember this daily and fully entrust our life's story to Him.

I am so thankful, Lord, that You are not confined in any sense. You work in realms that I know not of. And You work for my ultimate best. Thank You! I welcome You to direct every line, every moment, every scene in my life. Take care of all the "extras" too – those who are a part of my story in any way. Surround us with Your mighty presence, and I pray that our confidence in You will be firmly rooted and unmoved. Thank You for Your power and for Your genius! It's exciting to be Yours! Amen.

Just for me in **2 Kings**

18

Gaze Steady

Exodus 3:7-8, "*The Lord said, 'I have indeed seen the misery of My people in Egypt. I have heard them crying out because of their slave drivers, and I am concerned about their suffering. So I have come down to rescue them from the hand of the Egyptians and to bring them up out of that land into a good and spacious land, a land flowing with milk and honey—the home of the Canaanites, Hittites, Amorites, Perizzites, Hivites and Jebusites.'*"

God's eyes were on them. His ears were tuned to them. His heart was moved with concern about what He saw and heard. His people were suffering, and enough was enough!

This scene of suffering, however, was not new news or a short-term plight. Many people were born into, lived through, and died in slavery. These perplexing realities are nearly impossible to reconcile.

Tough as it was, God had shown His mighty hand and His loving heart along the way (Exodus 1:12, 17, 20-21; 2:9-10). Now, the time had come for Moses and Aaron to deliver this heaven-sent message: God is concerned about you. "And when they heard that the Lord was concerned about them and had seen their misery, they bowed down and worshiped" (Exodus 4:31). What a beautiful and fitting response!

Unfortunately, things got worse for them before they got better. By Exodus 6:9, the people were discouraged and distrusted God's promise all over again. It was hard for them to see any reason for hope as they looked at their now worse circumstances. Although they struggled to keep their eyes on God, God still kept His loving eye on them. He remained faithful. When the rescue mission was at last in full effect, God's people watched from a place of safety as plague after plague, God spared them from the suffering that devastated Egypt and ushered in their liberty.

Holding on to a distant hope in a difficult and distracting world is not any easier today. But, the beautiful heart of God can and *must* be trusted. He is looking at us and listening to us. We must return the gaze and give Him our full attention. He will do exactly what He says He will do. He has a plan for our greatest good, and He *will* bring us "into a good and spacious land."

Thank You, Lord, for being good through it all. You are the only dependable constant. Please bless me with a steady gaze, focused on You alone and not my circumstances. You are above it all, so I lift my eyes a little higher. I fix my eyes on You, unshakably, by Your grace. Amen.

Just for me in Exodus

19

By God Himself

Acts 7:34-35, "'I have indeed seen the oppression of My people in Egypt. I have heard their groaning and have come down to set them free. Now come, I will send you back to Egypt.' This is the same Moses they had rejected with the words, 'Who made you ruler and judge?' He was sent to be their ruler and deliverer by God Himself, through the angel who appeared to him in the bush."

This story first appears in Exodus. There, I was touched by the fact that God was moved with compassion based on what He saw and heard. Here in Acts the story is recounted – His people were groaning under oppression. God purposed that enough was enough and that He would set them free.

Here's the focal pivot: God calls a man. "Come, I will

send you back to Egypt." Not just any man, but Moses, the man whom an Israelite had years before looked at with scorn and asked, "Who made you the boss?" (Exodus 2:13-14). Well, this time the answer was clear: "God Himself."

Here's a fact: it really doesn't matter what happened in a prior season or what people may have thought. It doesn't matter if folks counted us out. God can very specifically turn that criticism around and use us in every way for which others thought we were unsuitable. No experience is wasted on God. He takes it all into account and fits us for our purpose even if we don't realize what's happening.

So, when people question us, but God has called us, or when it appears the task is complicated and messy, but the word from God is clear, we should root our confidence in the commentary that it was ordained "by God Himself." Whether or not anyone else can see what God is crafting, we should be confident knowing every strand in the tapestry of our lives is artfully designed by God Himself.

Help me, Lord, to live in full surrender to You and Your divine purposes for my life. Thank You for the fact that no one else's hang ups or opinions outweigh Your master plan. Therefore, help me never to get hung up on human criticism, doubts, or small thinking. That includes my own! Set me free from anything (even my-

self) that may be incarcerating my purpose and my potential. Perhaps You were setting Moses free just as much as You were freeing the Israelites. Wow, what a thought! Your purposes are vast and all-encompassing. May it be said that my story was lived as scripted by God Himself. In the name of Jesus I pray, Amen.

Just for me in *Acts*

20

A Matter of Power

1 Corinthians 2:13; 4:20, "This is what we speak, not in words taught us by human wisdom but in words taught by the Spirit, explaining spiritual realities with Spirit-taught words. . . . For the kingdom of God is not a matter of talk but of power."

A s I contemplate this verse, the wind is high and fiercely gusting. The typical serenity of the pre-dawn hour is interrupted by powerful, rushing winds, and I love it because it reminds me of God's power.

The kingdom of God is a matter of power. As I listen to the wind, I can't help but think of the mighty presence of the Holy Spirit at Pentecost and the demonstration of super-natural power that resulted (Acts 2:2-4). Literally, the words

the believers spoke that day were not human-taught, but en-
dowed by the Spirit. They spoke immediately in foreign lan-
guages that they had never learned, proclaiming with passion
and purpose a kingdom message that would reach the ends of
the earth. That's the power of God!

*So, do it in me! May my life reflect the evidence of Your power
in everything I do and say. I pray that I will be in tune with the
Spirit's teachings so that I can, in power, convey Your words as
You lead. In my daily orbitals, may Your mighty power accompany
me in an even greater measure than the forces of the wind. May
I flow in the power of the Holy Spirit. Teach me Your words, and
let Your power be seen. Amen.*

Just for me in **1 Corinthians**

21

God Will Be Their Teacher

Isaiah 54:13, "All your children will be taught by the Lord, and great will be their peace."

I remember this verse being shared with me by a lady who, with her husband, had raised two admirable children. This was the verse she claimed over them and repeated often so that they, too, knew and claimed this promise as theirs.

I love the idea of God Himself being my children's teacher. What a blessing to children and parents everywhere! God, who knows *everything* about *everyone* has the capacity, wisdom, and expertise to craft customized learning experiences for each unique individual. Indeed, all who live faithfully under His instruction are guaranteed a life of God-given peace.

Other similar verses complement this one:

Psalm 51:6, "Yet You desired faithfulness even in the womb; You taught me wisdom in that secret place."

Psalm 71:17, "Since my youth, God, You have taught me, and to this day I declare Your marvelous deeds."

Simply beautiful. Let's raise collective prayers for every child, born and unborn, that each one would be taught by the Lord Himself.

God, there is too much "us" in us that has the potential to be passed down to the next generation. But with You as our children's teacher, all wrongs will be made right and all weaknesses of character preemptively corrected. Only You are able to do this. It is a job too important for me. I pray that I will not get in Your way at any time, and that You would also continue to teach me and use me as You will. Thank You for these promises and affirmations in Your Word. My heart is grateful, relieved, and at peace. Amen.

Just for me in *Isaiah*

22

He's a Keeper

1 Thessalonians 5:23-24, "May God Himself, the God of peace, sanctify you through and through. May your whole spirit, soul and body be kept blameless at the coming of our Lord Jesus Christ. The One who calls you is faithful, and He will do it."

May God Himself (the one and only God for whom there is no substitute), "*the God of peace*" (the proprietor and generous distributor of unfathomable peace), "*sanctify you through and through*" (transform your entire being).

God is fully capable and willing to transform us! Not only can He do this, but He will *keep* us on this journey of sanctification until He comes, if we let Him. Let's not settle for a one-time experience with God's transforming power. May our commitment be to remain in the hands of our faithful God, the One who calls us to live a sanctified life. He is faithful, and He *will* do this lasting work in us.

Thank You, Lord. That last line is so compelling. You are able, You are faithful, and You will do it. Take my life in Your hands. Transform and keep me there. This I pray, in Jesus' wonderful name, Amen.

Just for me in **1 Thessalonians**

23

My Success Story

1 Samuel 18:14, "In everything he did he had great success, because the Lord was with him."

This verse is about David, but somewhere in the script of my life, I want this to be said of me. I want it to be a fact of every phrase and every line that the Lord is with me, that He is my constant companion and dependable guide. I want my life to bear evidence that He is my very best friend and greatest confidant. I want that connection to be obvious and attractive so that God alone is glorified.

Ultimately, I pray that my life's testimony would be the very same – in *everything* Kylah did, she had *great* success because the Lord was with her! I pray the very same for you.

Lord, first and foremost, I want You. May I never lose perspective and prioritize Your blessings over our relationship. That is primary. Thank You for being a God who promotes and provides pathways for my success. With every open door and higher height, may my relationship with You deepen. I pray, most of all, that this would be the greatest detail in my success story! Amen.

Just for me in **1 Samuel**

24

Forever Blessed

2 Samuel 7:28-29, *"Sovereign Lord, You are God! Your covenant is trustworthy, and You have promised these good things to Your servant. Now be pleased to bless the house of Your servant, that it may continue forever in Your sight; for You, Sovereign Lord, have spoken, and with Your blessing the house of Your servant will be blessed forever."*

When God makes a promise, He keeps His promise. His word is His bond. His "covenant is trustworthy." And, what's more, *all* of His promises are good. When I think of "good things," a few more texts come to mind:

Psalm 43:10, ". . . those who seek the Lord lack no good thing."

Psalm 84:11, ". . . the Lord bestows favor and honor; no good thing does He withhold from those whose walk is blameless."

Psalm 16:2, "I say to the Lord, You are my Lord; apart from You I have no good thing."

God is the giver of "every good and perfect gift" (James 1:17), and He can be trusted to lavish gifts and blessings beyond belief that are both personal and *lasting*. Nothing we can do for ourselves can compare to the reach, ability, and desire of God to bless us.

I want to remain forever under Your care, Lord. My heart is open to every good promise. Thank You for the eternal value of every blessing. This journey is exciting! You are amazing. I love You. Amen.

Just for me in *2 Samuel*

25

God Answers

Ezra 8:23, "*So we fasted and petitioned our God about this, and He answered our prayer.*"

I remember reading a quote once that said something like this: "Prayer is the power that moves the hand that moves the world." I love that! God gives us direct access to connect with Him in all of His mighty power. He is truly a prayer hearing and prayer answering God. Add to that what Jesus Himself told us about fasting (Matthew 17:19-21; Mark 9:29). Some things require the intentionality and sacrifice of fasting to translate petitions and intercessions into miraculous manifestations of God's exceeding power.

In Ezra's story, what drove him to fast and petition God

was a desire that God's glory would be seen. It was not of selfish ambition. He made certain claims about God before the king and he was not about to act in such a way that brought those claims into question. So, rather than rely on human wisdom and resources, Ezra, along with others, sought God intentionally and sacrificially for His name's sake, and God answered.

May my life testify to Your greatness, Lord! I trust that You are able to do literally anything. That includes everything I could never even think of. This tells me that I need to leave every unthinkable possibility in Your capable hands. I will seek You fervently and sacrificially to unleash the full extent of Your power in my life and in the lives of others. I want to magnify You in my life. Please continue to give me courage to press forward in faith and not to shrink back in fear or doubt. I am confident that this text will be on repeat in my catalogue of fresh testimonies. "So I fasted and petitioned my God about this, and He answered my prayer." Thank you, God. Amen.

Just for me in **Ezra**

26

Actions Speak Louder

1 Peter 2:15, "For it is God's will that by doing good you should silence the ignorant talk of foolish people."

Sometimes the thought of "God's will" seems big, intricate, complicated, and even illusive. I think that's why this verse struck me. In fact, it tickled me!

Get this. Scripture says it is actually God's will to get foolish people to shut up. How? By doing good, of course!

As funny as I find this, it really should be a guiding principle for every Christian. Not only the what, but also the how. Silence ignorance with benevolence.

The Bible gives plenty of commentary on how we should

choose and use our words. It truly is tempting to meet fire with fire or to get swept into debate about, essentially, foolishness. But here Peter (the wordiest disciple of them all) offers a direct, simple capture of what is also spoken of frequently in Proverbs and elsewhere in Scripture. Hand your actions the microphone. Let your good deeds do the talking. Soon enough the contest will be called in your favor.

Lord, this verse comes across so humorously, but it's not just humor. It's true. I want to do Your will in every way. Please give me the kind of resolve that prioritizes and has the patience to do good consistently – not letting unnecessary words get in the way – and so "silence the ignorant talk of foolish people." Thank you for this very clear revelation of Your will. Amen.

Just for me in 1 Peter

27

Consecration and Anticipation

Joshua 3:5, *"Joshua told the people, 'Consecrate yourselves, for tomorrow the Lord will do amazing things among you.'"*

Based on today's verse, here's what we should tell ourselves: *Live in a perpetual state of consecration so that every tomorrow can be bathed in anticipation that the Lord will do amazing things for us.*

What, then, does it mean to consecrate ourselves? Perhaps it looks like fully devoting ourselves to being used by God however He chooses. I am convinced, as the text reads, such a commitment yields an unrivaled thrill to life. Evidence of this materialized in the stories that followed.

Exhibit A: the crossing of the Jordan River (Joshua 3:15-17). God didn't part the waters as the children of Israel looked on from the shore. Instead, God moved as they moved. They had consecrated themselves and were primed to anticipate something "amazing." They stepped out in obedient faith. They were fully devoted and became active participants in this amazing miracle.

Not long after came exhibit B: the implosion of Jericho's impenetrable wall (Joshua 6:20). In lockstep, the consecrated men of Israel marched around the city in an unorthodox strategy, hinged on an obedient faith. Every day, with every step, they anticipated how God would move. God did not disappoint and secured an amazing victory for them.

So Lord, show me what it truly means to consecrate myself. Show me how to live in a perpetual state of consecration. I want that eager sense of anticipation that You are up to something major to be a regular feature in my life. Sensitize my heart to every one of Your amazing acts in and around me. I want You to be unrestrained to do impossible, mind-blowing, amazing things in my life. I'm ready for the thrill! Amen.

Just for me in *Joshua*

28

Tasteful Talking

Colossians 4:6, *"Let your conversation be always full of grace, seasoned with salt, so that you may know how to answer everyone."*

It is not easy to maintain a graceful tone or gracious answer, especially when faced with the likes of defensiveness, dismissiveness, or disrespect. And when incessant interrogation, false accusations, and faulty assumptions enter the picture . . . *did I say it's not the easiest?*

But this text challenges us to keep grace on our tongues! Take a pause, learn to listen, and answer graciously as we would want done to us. That's in every situation. Always speak tastefully. Without a doubt, this is a game-changing standard to live by.

Help me, Lord! This is a principle I am trying to master by Your good grace. The truth is, You've brought me far on this mouth-minding journey. I still have a ways to go! I do believe with all my heart that great growth and maturity is packaged in mastering this principle. This, by Your grace, will form part of my testimony. Thank You even now! Amen.

Just for me in Colossians

29

Brand Your Brilliance

1 Timothy 4:14, "*Do not neglect your gift, which was given you through prophecy when the body of elders laid their hands on you.*"

Tonight, I was scrolling through my emails, doing a purge of the latest subscription-based messages. As I did, one subject line caught my attention: "Brand Your Brilliance." I didn't read the entire message. I didn't register for the "master class." However, the catchy title got me thinking about 1 Timothy 4:14. In essence, this scripture says don't shrink back from using your God-given gift – what others see and affirm in you. Do not set it aside. Embrace it! Use it! Walk in it!

A brand is a clearly recognizable symbol, look, or color

that conveys a large message in a simple way. The brilliance we carry is a branded billboard for the excellence of our great God! So, step up to the plate with all of your God-gifted talent and ability, and *shine!*

God, please attach boldness and courage to the gifts You have given me. I pray that they will flourish under Your care. Open my eyes and my heart to opportunities and avenues to express Your good gifts. Surround me with people who see the gifts of God in me and will walk with me on the journey through prayer and encouragement. Thank You for this reminder that my gifts are from You, and they should be used to glorify You. Amen.

Just for me in **1 Timothy**

30

Blessings on Blessings!

Haggai 2:8-9, "'The silver is Mine and the gold is Mine,' declares the Lord Almighty. 'The glory of this present house will be greater than the glory of the former house,' says the Lord Almighty. 'And in this place I will grant peace,' declares the Lord Almighty.*"

What a necessary reminder on so many levels! God has a greater future planned for us, *and* He has unlimited resources to bring it to pass. He is able to do immeasurably more than our capacity to imagine (Ephesians 3:20). We must recall this promise regularly and embrace it as a statement of fact.

The blessing of peace is a sweet cherry on top. Only God can do something like that. No need for striving or stressing.

Instead, we must plug into God's plan and timing. We must anchor our trust in Him alone and forget about our own limits. Everything belongs to Him. What limits and stumps us has no such effect on Him. Following His lead, we will be blessed by His provision, His plan, and His peace.

I pray for all of this, God. And I pray that, just as in Ephesians 3:20-21, You will be eternally glorified as the all-powerful One who is more than able to exceed every one of my expectations, using me in the process. What an awesome God You truly are! I bless Your name God, and I thank You for this and every other promise that I can claim as mine. I pray this with gratitude and anticipation. Amen.

Just for me in *Haggai*

31

My God and Me

Amos 4:13, "He who forms the mountains, who creates the wind, and who reveals His thoughts to mankind, who turns dawn to darkness, and treads on the heights of the earth—the Lord God Almighty is His name."

God is all-powerful. He is larger than the grandeur of lofty mountains. He is capable of routing the wind. Consistent and punctual, He brings to pass day and night. The earth itself is His footstool. That's our God. He is perfect, just, faithful, and upright. "He is the Rock" (Deuteronomy 32:4). The Lord God Almighty is His name. He is worthy to be praised based solely on who He is.

Yet, smack in the middle of this awe-inspiring picture of

God, bookended by His excellence, is a snapshot of God in relation to us. This great God reveals His thoughts to mankind. That is a wow factor without a doubt. There is so much that we just don't know or understand, but our all-powerful God is willing to reveal His thoughts to us.

This is a powerful and almost overwhelming thought, but God, I am thankful for the revelations You provide. I am open. Fill me up. Enlighten me. Expand Your power in my life. Thank You, Jesus, even now. Amen.

Just for me in *Amos*

32

Head Gear

Obadiah 1:15, "*The day of the Lord is near for all nations. As you have done, it will be done to you; your deeds will return upon your own head.*"

"What have you *done?*" That question can strike the heart with terror. The mind begins to race, filtering through deeds to figure out what could have been so offensive as to provoke that question.

But pause. What *have* you done?

Take a deep breath and reflect. Anything excellent? Praiseworthy? Of good report? Have you been striving in a positive direction? The time will come when "as you have done, it will be done to you."

Just envision, if your deeds returning "upon your own head" became a literal headpiece! Would you be embarrassed with your head weighted down in misery, or would you stride with stylish confidence? You will not escape your actions nor your treatment of others, so walk circumspectly and always do to others what would translate beautifully into good fashion for you.

Lord, I always want to easily hold my head up. So let my deeds honor and glorify You. I pray that goodness alone will rest on me. Amen.

Just for me in **Obadiah**

33

What Do You Expect?

Philippians 1:19-20, *"For I know that through your prayers and God's provision of the Spirit of Jesus Christ what has happened to me will turn out for my deliverance. I eagerly expect and hope that I will in no way be ashamed, but will have sufficient courage so that now as always Christ will be exalted in my body, whether by life or by death."*

What has happened to me will turn out for my deliverance." What a powerful, confident expression of faith! We've all experienced the full range of good and bad happenings in our lives, some more intense than others. When bad things happen, it can feel crushing. We often carry the residual impact into the future and find that we are never quite the same.

Rather than sinking under the weight of this reality, I love the perspective in this text. Yes, it happened; yet, in answer to every prayer and by the presence of the Holy Spirit Himself, it *will* work out for my ultimate good. Based on that, I will courageously hope with great expectation that God will be glorified by my life's testimony.

Now, let's address expectations. Sometimes we have vague or low expectations of God when He is more than willing and fully able to meet and exceed our loftiest expectations of Him. Out of our pain we minimize our hopes, and for fear of disappointment we often do not express our heart's desire at all. We sit in shame and venture nothing. Let's shift that paradigm. Instead, let's endeavor to be fully vulnerable and shamelessly expectant of what God can do through us, however He chooses to do it, for His glory.

God, I am expecting great things from You! I am deeply grateful for every prayer ever prayed for me and for the provision of the Holy Spirit. I am thankful for the reminder that high expectations do not have to be extinguished by painful experiences. Instead, I can take courage and boldly declare that by Your Spirit it will work out. It will result in a better version of me. It will very clearly glorify You, making it easy for others to see what a mighty, excellent, fully capable, loving God I serve. Whether I live or die, please be fully glorified through me for who You are and how You can make something beautiful out of any mess. You are a great God, and You can be fully trusted! Thank You, God. I'm choosing to live with eager expectation. Amen.

Just for me in *Philippians*

34

Lover and Leader

Nehemiah 9:19, *"Because of Your great compassion You did not abandon them in the wilderness. By day the pillar of cloud did not fail to guide them on their path, nor the pillar of fire by night to shine on the way they were to take."*

God's character is impressive and beautiful in every way. I pray that thoughts of who God is in our lives and what He is capable of would prevail in our minds daily. I pray that this would be our driving force and reassuring anchor. Because He has such a heart of love, we can be confident that He will never abandon us. According to His very promise, He will, in fact, never leave us nor forsake us (Hebrews 13:5). He is a faithful God, and that resonates loudly in today's verse.

The people spoken of in this text, the newly emancipated Israelites, were completely reliant on God. Or I should say, they *needed* to be completely reliant on God.

Out there in the wilderness they had not a clue about which way to go, how to remain safe, or much of anything about wilderness living for that matter. To rely on themselves would be a death sentence. Although their gratitude and acknowledgment of this was not always on point, their faithful God stuck with them and "did not fail to guide them on their path."

We ought not take God's compassion, provision, protection, guidance, or faithfulness for granted. What's more, we need not be fickle or inconsistent in our reliance on God by choosing to rely on ourselves. That is literally a recipe for small living and ultimate disaster! We must avail ourselves to the consistent, day-by-day, moment-by-moment guidance of God in our lives. By the grace of God, we will remain aware and in awe of His great compassion.

Thank You, God, for gracing us with the essence of You. All Your wonderful attributes are praiseworthy and keep me in awe. I invite You, in all Your fullness, to lead me and love me. I don't want to go a moment without Your presence in my life. Tune my heart to You. Keep my eyes on You. May I come to experience more and more of You. Amen.

Just for me in *Nehemiah*

35

My Story for Your Glory

Mark 5:19, *"Jesus did not let him, but said, 'Go home to your own people and tell them how much the Lord has done for you, and how He has had mercy on you.'"*

People need to know what God can do. There is so much confusion, speculation, and misinformation floating around. As a result, many people are ignorant of or resistant to the fact that Jesus is the answer to every problem. He is able to see us through every difficulty and seeming impossibility. He is limitless. He is generous. He blesses and provides in ways that we do not ask, do not notice, and cannot possibly count. He is amazing!

The people in Mark 5 did not see this. Jesus had just

transformed a tormented life. The once crazed man, having encountered Jesus, sat dignified, marveling at his new-found liberty. Arriving on the scene of freedom, however, the town's people were bound to their sense of normalcy. In stark contrast to the man liberated from demonic possession, they pleaded with Jesus "to leave their region" (v. 17). They possessed a sad comfort level with demonic company and a strange discomfort with the life-giving, powerful presence of Jesus.

Jesus honored their request. He departed, but He still cared. The man was eager to follow his Liberator. Instead, Jesus granted him the challenging opportunity to stay where he was and to testify about what God had done. Perhaps this was just as much for the man's journey to wholeness as it was to reach the unbelieving. Jesus commissioned him, "Speak about it. Tell what God has done. Don't let your testimony die."

Jesus needed the people to become acquainted with what true freedom and transformation looked and sounded like. By the mercy of God, this one freed man put the transforming power of God on display. "And all the people were amazed" (v. 20).

Lord, it really is amazing what You can do! Thank You for Your transforming power and for seeing the big picture at all times. Thank You for redeeming my fragmented past and using me to put Your mighty power and kindness on display. I pray that I will follow Your instructions even when my desire seems right. You want to accomplish so much more than I could possibly fathom. Help me to trust You. Help me to be obedient. Help me to go where You say go. Help me to say what You want me to say. Use my story for Your glory. This I pray, in Jesus' name, Amen.

Just for me in *Mark*

36

Lord, Would You Train My Brain?

Romans 8:6, *"The mind governed by the flesh is death, but the mind governed by the Spirit is life and peace."*

A devotional thought I read this morning emphasized that circumstances are not our actual problem. Often, it's more mindset than circumstance. If that is so, it must hold true that outlook can lift the weight of circumstances. This is precisely why we must offer our minds to be governed and transformed by the Spirit.

"The mind governed by the flesh is death." Does anything sound good about that? No matter how clever, level-headed, or analytical we think we are, relying on our own logic does not end well. It ends quite tragically in fact. We will think ourselves into a corner and then act dumbfounded wondering how we got there.

"But the mind governed by the Spirit is life and peace." This is it. This is what we all want: a thriving life characterized by peace of heart and mind. This is only possible with the Spirit at the helm. He simultaneously filters the thoughts that rob us of life and peace and instills that which connects us to the heart and mind of God.

As we navigate this world that bombards us with circumstance after heavy circumstance, let's commit our minds to be "governed by the Spirit."

So yes, Lord. I ask with all sincerity that You take up permanent residence as Captain of my thought life. Flood my mind with that which affords daily peace. Tame my flesh. Give me a resounding victory. I want to experience the fullness of life in You. That is only possible with the governing activity of Your Spirit. I grant You full access with no term limits. Come in today. Come in to stay! Thank You, Jesus. Amen.

Just *for me in* Romans

37

Deep Work

Ezekiel 36:26-27, "I will give you a new heart and put a new spirit in you; I will remove from you your heart of stone and give you a heart of flesh. And I will put My Spirit in you and move you to follow My decrees and be careful to keep My laws."

There is no doubt about it; we need the Spirit's activity in our lives. Hands down. No questions asked. He is able to change the deepest parts within us. He is able to make us sensitive to and more keenly aware of what He has purposed as best for us to do.

I love that God doesn't leave us to "will or do" on our own (Philippians 2:13). He is willing and able to literally place desire, drive, and longing in our hearts, so that we are compelled toward and intent on living to honor Him. He alone can restore the Christlike spirit that He built us to manifest.

Here I am, Lord. I'll sign up as a primary candidate for Your skillful work. I need it. I want it. Take my heart, and do Your perfect work in me. I love You, and I am thankful. Amen.

Just for me in Ezekiel

38

Steady and Strong

Habakkuk 3:19, *"The Sovereign Lord is my strength; He makes my feet like the feet of a deer, He enables me to tread on the heights."*

The Sovereign Lord *is* my strength." This scripture is written in the present tense and exemplifies that the strength the Lord provides is continuous: today, every day.

This is a promise full of reassurance. He is our strength in new and unfamiliar territory. He is our stability. And let's not forget, He is sovereign. He is ruler over all, orchestrator of all, strategist of all, working things out through it all. He knows every one of our needs, our aptitudes, and our struggles.

Taking all of this into account, He personalizes the

strength and stability He offers – physically, mentally, emotionally, professionally, and spiritually. He is *my* strength. He makes *my* feet. He enables *me*.

Yes, we should take this very personally. We should trust that this promise is eternally ours. Why? Because as Hebrews 13:8 says, "Jesus Christ is the same yesterday, today, and forever."

Thank You, Lord. I accept this promise as mine. I cannot operate without the strength You provide. There are heights You have in mind for me, and I want to scale them. Only with You is that even remotely possible, and certainly sustainable by You alone. For today, and every "today" to come, I embrace the strength and stability You provide. I feel empowered to face every task with confidence, knowing that the Source of my strength never expires. That's good news. Great news! Amen.

Just for me in *Habakkuk*

39

Every Single Thing

Genesis 6:22, "Noah did everything just as God commanded him."

What God said, Noah did. Everything. Step-by-step. There was no common-sense rationale or pre-existing context for the instructions given. The validity rested entirely in the One who gave them. For Noah, understanding was not primary; relationship and trust were. Thus, the testimony was given, "Noah did everything just as God commanded him."

What an inspiration! Can this be my testimony too? "Kylah did everything just as God commanded her." I like the sound of that! Go ahead. Place your name in there.

Like Noah, we should resolve to trust God implicitly, and to obey Him readily. In the face of the unbelievable, the unlikely, the confusing, the odd, the complicated, the unforeseen, or anything else, we, too, can cultivate a relationship with Him that is secure and a trust in Him that is unwavering.

The sentiment of complete trust is beautifully summarized in this quote on Christian living:

> Holiness . . . is an entire surrender of the will to God; it is living by every word that proceeds from the mouth of God; it is doing the will of our heavenly Father; it is trusting God in trial, in darkness as well as in the light; it is walking by faith and not by sight; it is relying on God with unquestioning confidence, and resting in His love.[2]

May the record of our lives show that we lived in full surrender and carried out every single thing that God said.

Only by Your strength, God. Only by Your grace. Help me to be this in tune with Your will — fully surrendered and obedient at all times. Be my Lord, my God, and my Teacher. May I be a star pupil, and do everything just as You say. Amen.

Just for me in **Genesis**

40

Pride Aside

Esther 4:17, *"So Mordecai went away and carried out all of Esther's instructions."*

At the height of the saga recorded in Esther, the Jews were in significant trouble. The king's arbitrary decree for their destruction and death sent shockwaves ripping through every Jewish home. Distraught, Mordecai put his grief on full display – weeping and wailing, mourning and fasting, clothed in sackcloth and ashes. In his condition, he could not approach the palace. Help was just beyond his reach.

The spectacle of Mordecai's demonstrative grief, however, soon reached a stunned Esther. She urgently sent for word from him. Finally able to get a message through, Mordecai sent her specific instructions: ask, beg, *plead* for mercy from the king on behalf of the Jews. Mordecai urged Esther to see the providence in her position. Unlike the unquestioning obedience to Mordecai's every word until then (Esther 2:20, 22), Esther broke the trend and sent a message back. This time she had instructions for Mordecai.

Here's where the story could have gone completely awry. Imagine if Mordecai took a posture of spiritual snobbery. Imagine if he refused to see that God could use Esther in this way too. Imagine if he was unwilling to invite the Jewish people into partnership with God for their deliverance. "Remember, Esther, it was my God-fearing investment that groomed you to be where you are today. Will you really doubt my instruction?" Imagine the horror that could have resulted from such a prideful posture.

Esther's request to call her people to fast could only have come from God. Mordecai had a choice: to participate in or to stand in the way of God's plan. He chose the former. If Mordecai arrogantly believed that God spoke one direction- ally – through him to Esther and never the other way around – he would have missed the move of God that reached be- yond the power he saw in the palace to the power she saw up above. Thankfully, Mordecai put any pride aside and cooperated with how God moved through Esther.

God, please tune me in to Your voice. Fill me with Your Spirit so that I will discern when You are speaking, no matter the messenger. Remind me when I forget. Remind me when I cling to an expectation or a preference to only hear directly from You. Give me the clarity and the confidence to know whenever You are speaking. For even an indirect word, if it's from You, is enough. Amen.

Just *for me in* Esther

41

Hope. Seek. Wait.

Lamentations 3:25-26, *"The Lord is good to those whose hope is in Him, to the one who seeks Him; it is good to wait quietly for the salvation of the Lord."*

When we live in hopeful expectation, intentionally seeking after God, we are regularly reminded of this fact: the Lord is good, so good to us! At times, however, we impatiently rush ahead, and try to operate without God. Other times, we foolishly second-guess Him. We place our hopes in what our natural eyes can see. We seek our own desires and call them God's desires. We ultimately put God's richest blessings for us at risk when we fail to be still and to wait.

Yes, the Lord is good to us. But let's remember, our opportunity to reflect His good heart comes when we wait patiently for His best work in our lives. What God has for us will always outshine what "good" we could manufacture on our own.

Hope in Him – have high expectations.

Seek Him – make your pursuit intentional.

Wait for Him – be confident that He is there even in the wait, and trust that what's on the other side of the wait is absolutely worth it!

Jesus, my hope is in You. I will seek after You. I will wait on You. By Your grace and goodness, I will experience the fullness of You and Your desires for me now and for eternity. Keep me focused, hopeful, and seeking even in the waiting. Amen.

Just for me in *Lamentations*

42

Let Me Tell You 'Bout My Friend!

Song of Songs 5:10, 16, "My beloved is radiant and ruddy, outstanding among ten thousand. . . . His mouth is sweetness itself; he is altogether lovely. This is my beloved, this is my friend, daughters of Jerusalem."

Doesn't this text make you smile? Brag on him, sis!

Woven into this young woman's gushing words of affirmation is a practice worthy of emulation. Every now and then we ought to take a pause and publicly celebrate the people God has gifted to us.

In fact, will you indulge me as I join her?

God did something special when He blessed me with my husband. Before I prayed and *as* I prayed, God chiseled this one out just for me. If I could borrow a few words, he is "outstanding among ten thousand." Handsome. Intelligent. Eloquent. Admirable. Romantic. Hilarious. Talented. Well-rounded. Attentive. Patient. Creative. Adventurous. Ambitious. Helpful. Thoughtful. Passionate. Intentional. Spiritual.

My beloved. My friend.

Listen, I *must* invite you to join in too. Who brings love and joy into your life? Your spouse? A family member? A forever friend? Tell them. Tell *everybody*. Let there be no question of who they are, just how special they are in your eyes, and what they mean to you.

You in? Let's put it out there. Let's spread a few smiles.

Thank You, Lord, for the beauty and blessing of God-given, God-ordained relationships. Please put words in my mouth and an impulse in my heart to regularly celebrate those who have enriched my life so tremendously. May I always remember that You are the source. I pray these things with gratitude, in Jesus' name, Amen.

Just for me in Song of Songs

43

When You Move, I Move

Numbers 9:22-23, "*Whether the cloud stayed over the tabernacle for two days or a month or a year, the Israelites would remain in camp and not set out; but when it lifted, they would set out. At the Lord's command they encamped, and at the Lord's command they set out. They obeyed the Lord's order, in accordance with His command through Moses.*"

The Israelites modeled an excellent posture that I pray the Lord will perfect in you and in me. When He moved, they moved. Nothing about the operation was predictable except this: the cloud of His presence was always there, and at some point, the cloud would move. It could be one day (v. 21), two days, a month, or a year. That's quite a range, to say the least. Thus, it was in their best interest to remain in a state of readiness and reliance. The same is true of us.

I want this kind of obedience to be the theme of my life. The kind where it doesn't matter what God says, but that *He* said it. When God says to stay, *stay!* When God says to go, *go!* When God says to move, *move!* As we keep in step with the leadership of God, we can expect to experience every amazing blessing that He has promised as the fruit of that kind of lifestyle.

Lord, give me the resolve and depth of trust not to run ahead or lag behind. May my focus remain on You. Please help me to remain consistent in following Your lead. Whether I sit in a season of waiting, or experience a swift turnaround, I pray that I will obey and willingly move when You say move. Lead me, Lord. I will follow. Amen.

Just for me in *Numbers*

44

God's Got This!

Nahum 1:9*, "Whatever they plot against the Lord He will bring to an end; trouble will not come a second time."*

The bottom line of Nahum 1:9 is this: we need to remain on the Lord's side. God is all-powerful and all-knowing. Nothing can overwhelm or surprise Him. Nothing is outside of His control. He is patient and loving and fair, and this reveals itself differently, depending on how we position ourselves in relation to Him.

Let's backtrack a few verses. Nahum 1:3 describes God as patient and powerful, but also able to inflict punishment where punishment is due. Similarly, verses 7-8 tell us that He is good, that He provides protection, and that He cares, while also making it plain that His enemies don't stand a chance against Him. So, there are two expressions of God's goodness and greatness represented here: one that nurtures and protects and one that does not prevent, but rather inflicts destruction.

That brings us back to verse 9 and invokes the question: Why persist in stubbornness? Schemes against the Lord are futile. Plans that don't align with His will are foolish. They will cause a good round of trouble, and at some point, in some way, God will bring them to a final end.

So, what is the best choice? Let's choose to live under the divine direction and protection of God. Let's allow Him deal with the trouble in our lives. The Lord is great in power (v. 3), He is good, He is a refuge, and He cares (v. 7). Why stand in opposition to a God like that? Let's remain squarely on His side, and let Him fight to make things right.

Thank You, Lord, for who You are: a force of love and power against whom no one and nothing can stand. I entrust myself completely to You. Amen.

Just for me in *Nahum*

45

My God *Will* Hear Me

Micah 7:7, *"But as for me, I watch in hope for the Lord, I wait for God my Savior; my God will hear me."*

It's that last statement of confidence that really anchors this text for me. "My God *will* hear me." With all of the talk about mindset, positivity, and self-talk, this verse leaps off the page as one to embrace as a daily mantra. It doesn't matter what things look like in a natural sense. The world and everything in it may be going completely crazy. At times there are more unanswered questions and unfulfilled desires than I care to admit.

But . . .

As for me . . .

I watch in hope for the Lord . . .

I wait for God my Savior . . .

My God WILL hear me!

"This is the confidence we have in approaching God," 1 John 5:14-15 affirms. Whatever we ask, according to His will, we *know* we have!

God, I praise You! No good thing will You withhold from those whose walk is upright (Psalm 84:11). You will hear me. I watch and wait in great anticipation of what You will do. I praise You, God! Amen.

Just for me in Micah

46

Focus on God. Imitate Good.

3 John 1:11, "*Dear friend, do not imitate what is evil but what is good. Anyone who does what is good is from God. Anyone who does what is evil has not seen God.*"

How we operate on a consistent basis is a tell-tale sign of where our attention lies. We have a tendency to replicate what we focus on.

The question is: Are you looking up or looking around?

Let's be honest and admit together that there is a very real temptation to "imitate what is evil." I mean, sometimes it's tough to walk the straight and narrow, take the high road, or take one for the team, isn't it? At times we find ourselves protecting self because "everyone else" is protecting self. We adopt the posture of "getting mine" and "looking out for me." We pretend as if life is perfect. We give less, take more, and withhold grace.

Look around, and you'll find a steady feed of material to keep you distracted and reactive.

Not only does that sound exhausting, but it also reveals a profoundly sad reality. By getting caught up in looking around, we fail to truly see God for who He is and what He is capable of through *good works*. What we think we might gain in doing what is evil is merely a blinding façade. A clear vision of God will be more than a motivating factor towards striving to imitate His way and none other. His resumé lays out the winning way.

The admonition in 3 John 1:11 dispels the notion that we must meet fire with fire. Instead, we must stay in tune with God, gain our marching orders from Him, and imitate His example of what is good. This accomplishes more than we ever could any other way. The one who does good is from God, and with God as the source, the possibilities are limitless.

Lord, I have seen You and the good things You do. That is motivating enough for me to say today that I want to imitate Your good way. Right now, in this beautiful and peaceful time with You,

Lord, I pray that this will translate into my day-to-day living. When the temptation comes to match the heat and take matters into my own hands, help me to set self aside and fully experience You in the good that You can empower me to do. Only by Your power and grace am I able. Thank You even now! Amen.

Just for me in 3 John

47

An Abundance of Favor

Leviticus 26:9-10, *"'I will look on you with favor and make you fruitful and increase your numbers, and I will keep My covenant with you. You will still be eating last year's harvest when you will have to move it out to make room for the new.'"*

Let me tell you what. God is so supremely generous. He is both able and willing to supply our every need according to His unfathomable riches (Philippians 4:19). He blesses in unmistakable ways that leave an identifying mark and a lasting impression that denote "God was here." These "God markers" come in all forms. They look like circumstances and provision and timing and protection and insight and resources and promptings (really, I could go on) that very clearly could have only come from God.

To experience the fullness of God's promised blessings, He invites us into relationship with Him. He invites us to *trust* Him. We see this in Leviticus 26. Life in Egypt had been a bad situation for the Israelites. Now free, they were plunged into a new reality. God, with a heart full of love, spoke to all of Israel through Moses, conveying the optimal lifestyle and establishing rules for this new nation. It was unfamiliar, but it was best. God was setting them up for an abundance of favor. Their duty was simple: trust and obey. Our duty is the same.

As our Creator, God knows the circumstances under which we thrive. He presents them to us and invites us to sign up for the abundant favor and the thrilling adventure that comes along with living by His design. Psalm 34:9-10 frames it perfectly. "Fear the Lord, you His holy people, for those who fear Him lack nothing. The lions may grow weak and hungry, but those who seek the Lord lack no good thing."

Lord, I claim the promise of today's verse as my very own. I claim increase, abundance, and favor. My heart is open to every blessing You have in mind for me. Prepare me, Lord. Give me a resolve to say yes to You in word and in deed. My hope and expectations are high, but never as high as what You have in store. Your thoughts and ways are always higher than mine. You are capable of do-

ing far more than I could ever ask or imagine, even on my most creative days. God, I want my life's story to abound with "God markers" and clear evidences of Your favor. Do what You must in me so that I can experience Your fullness. I'm excited Lord, and I am thankful. I love You. In Jesus' name I pray, Amen.

Just for me in *Leviticus*

48

God Bless You

Ruth 2:12, "*May the Lord repay you for what you have done. May you be richly rewarded by the Lord, the God of Israel, under whose wings you have come to take refuge.*"

The landscape of our lives is adorned with beautiful, bountiful blessings that God often lavishes through ordinary people. I'm sure we could craft quite the list. Here are the two things I want us to do next time a willing vessel applies a God-ordained blessing to our lives.

First, take a moment to acknowledge the source: "The God of Israel." It is because of His kindness that anyone can be kind. It is because of His generosity that anyone be generous. He is the originator of every good thing (James 1:17).

Then, extend prayers of reciprocal blessings for those God has used to bless us. Pray that they experience Him too. Pray that God will take a personal interest in repaying and richly rewarding them as only He can. With all sincerity breathe this timeless prayer: "God bless you."

God, I thank You because You have blessed me in innumerable ways through the hands of people, vessels used by You. I pray blessings and favor and right reward over them, Lord. Flood their lives with every good thing. Above all, anchor them in connection with You. May they acknowledge You as the source of every good and perfect gift. May this motivate them to do Your bidding and remain in relationship with You. For those who have not consciously yielded their will, my prayer is that they will come to know and experience the thrill of connection with the mighty, compassionate, life-transforming God whom it has been my pleasure to experience. Thank You, God, for the vastness of You. There is more than enough at Your disposal to go around infinitely. As I have been and continue to be so richly blessed, I pray personal, tailor-made blessings for others in return. For Your excellent greatness, today and forever, I thank You. Amen.

Just for me in **Ruth**

49

Nothing Better. Best Thing Ever!

Ecclesiastes 3:12, *"I know that there is nothing better for people than to be happy and to do good while they live."*

Be happy. Do good.

Do good. Be happy.

Either way you put it, we are told that doing good and being happy are the best things ever! In fact, the two are mutually informing. Once you are happy, doing good easily follows. Once you do good, a good dose of "happy" floods in. You can't lose! We have one shot at life on this earth, and while we live it, let's take this wisdom to heart.

Lord, this makes me smile and it enlarges a desire in me "to be happy and to do good." When I don't feel so happy, supply Your Spirit and give me an unshakable urge to do good. As joy takes residence, I pray that mine would be a compounding experience of happiness and goodness – on cycle, on repeat. This is Your ideal for me, and I'm grateful. Thank You, Jesus! Amen.

Just for me in *Ecclesiastes*

50

When Grace Follows You

Jonah 3:1, "Then the word of the Lord came to Jonah a second time."

D id you catch the grace in this text? What a good, patient, forgiving God we serve. He is willing to take risks on us despite our frailties and faults. This verse comes after quite an episode. Jonah 1:1 introduces the drama this way: "The word of the Lord came to Jonah son of Amittai." In response to that word, Jonah exits stage left and does his own thing. He goes in the complete opposite direction, nearly dies, and ends up sticky and smelly in fish vomit on a beach somewhere.

That was the first time.

The truth is, many of us would give such a person no future opportunity to complete the mission. Jonah showed his colors very clearly!

But enter grace: "Then the word of the Lord came to Jonah a second time." If this isn't evidence of God's grace, I don't know what is. This is good news! God isn't quick to cut us loose or cancel our usefulness for Him. He has a big heart and sees through our defenses, insecurities, prejudices, and ignorance. He sees someone who can be transformed even as He uses us. Even when we act on our own terms, as if we know what is best and He does not, He is not above sending us a word a second time.

When God speaks, even in view of His grace, let it be our posture to listen the first time! No hesitation or delay! I am grateful for all that "the second time" represents of God. Yet, how much grief could be spared and how much more peace could be experienced if, on round one, we choose to keep in step with the Spirit?

Lord, I relish thoughts of hearing from You; however, I don't always think forward to the "what if" of difficult follow through. Empower me by Your Spirit, Lord. May I respond with fervor and immediacy to whatever You say. Where I have been slow or disobedient, thank You for Your grace. I trust You, God. Speak to my heart today. Amen.

Just for me in *Jonah*

51

I'm Yours to the Last Drop

Zephaniah 1:12, *"At that time I will search Jerusalem with lamps and punish those who are complacent, who are like wine left on its dregs, who think, 'The Lord will do nothing, either good or bad.'"*

A re we complacent? Do we have more to give, yet rest on our laurels? If so, I dare say this may betray an underlying belief that God is an inactive, disinterested God.

This does not represent who God is. God is not inactive nor disinterested. Instead, He actively seeks and hopes for diligence and alertness in us. As a people who serve God as living sacrifices, we can never say we have arrived. We can never say we have done all that we must do. God gives more than a hint that He desires our ongoing investment, partnership, and activity in His work (Matthew 25:34-40).

Complacency and dismissive flippancy will absolutely yield painful punishment and separation from God. As long as we are breathing, we must expend our energies, gifts, talents, resources, and even our creativity – *everything* – in congruence with our belief that God is both active in our lives and interested in our offering.

So, I pray that my heart remains stirred, that in no way will I settle complacently and behave as if I have nothing left to give. Lord, be the husbandman. Extract every drop of what You nurtured in me for Your eternal glory. This I pray in Your name, Amen.

Just for me in *Zephaniah*

52

When God Gives Gifts

1 Kings 4:29, "God gave Solomon wisdom and very great insight, and a breadth of understanding as measureless as the sand on the seashore."

Talk about a triple threat! I must admit, I've read and attached God's generous blessing of Solomon to wisdom alone, but as I read again, slowly and intentionally, those "ands" jumped out at me. God gave him wisdom, *and* great insight, *and* measureless understanding. That is amazing! We see this awe in the verses that follow when people from everywhere showed up to see if it were so.

"How could one person know so much and have proficiency in such diverse subject matter?"

"Who has the time to study all of that?"

"How is it that sound wisdom is always on the tip of his tongue?"

I'm sure these and more questions were swirling around in the minds of many. The answer: only God can give such gifts.

I'm thankful, Lord, and I open my heart to be filled by You. I pray that every ounce of every gift You have chosen to give to me will be used in full measure to magnify You. Lord, I pray for extraordinary impact through the gifts You've given and will give. Thank You for what You are doing through me even now. I am forever Yours. Amen.

Just for me in *1 Kings*

53

In Strength

Judges 6:14, *"The Lord turned to him and said, 'Go in the strength you have and save Israel out of Midian's hand. Am I not sending you?'"*

That last statement is what really grips my heart. "Am I not sending you?" Don't you get it? You do realize Who is sending you, right? This is our singular and sufficient assurance despite the apparent odds.

This verse alone backs up popular phrases like, "whom God calls He enables" or "God equips those He calls." We ought to believe this and live with anticipation of just how God will accomplish His plans and purposes for us, especially when things look impossible, insurmountable, out of reach, or above our pay grade.

Lean in and hear God say, "Am I not sending you?" Smile, knowing that this is all you need. When He says go in the strength you have, know that everything will be alright because your strength is in Him! He *is* your strength! He will bring to pass whatever He has put in your heart.

Thank You, God, for being my strength and for using me to do more than I could ever do without You. Here I am. Send me! Amen.

Just for me in *Judges*

54

Knowledge is Power

2 Peter 1:2-3, "*Grace and peace be yours in abundance through the knowledge of God and of Jesus our Lord. His divine power has given us everything we need for a godly life through our knowledge of Him who called us by His own glory and goodness.*"

Knowledge. It's referenced twice in this text, reiterated for our benefit. Exactly *what* knowledge is so key? The text tells us it's the "knowledge of God."

Head knowledge? Maybe.

Heart knowledge? Definitely.

This "knowledge" of God refers to an intimate connection with Him. As we grow in greater depth and connection, grace and peace can indeed be enjoyed in abundance.

Furthermore, we can avail of every aid God has to offer, not to mention His immense power, to live a life instructed by and ultimately pleasing to Him.

Get close to Him. Go deep with Him. Love Him. Let Him love you fully. An abundant life of grace and peace awaits. Living a godly life is completely possible. It's all available through His divine power which comes plentifully packaged in knowing Him personally. Nothing is worth more!

Father, I want to know You and live every day through the filter of that knowledge. Thank You for grace, peace, power, and provision. I love You and want to love You more! Amen.

Just for me in 2 Peter

55

One Voice Matters

Galatians 1:15-16, *"But when God, who set me apart from my mother's womb and called me by His grace, was pleased to reveal His Son in me so that I might preach Him among the Gentiles, my immediate response was not to consult any human being."*

When God says go, *go!* What He says do, *do!* His plan for you was conceived before you were. His word is supreme. Up against His word, other opinions do not matter! When people ask why, and should they offer to show you a "better way," point upward and inward. He is the Master Strategist. Trust His word over your life. Stand on that firm, unshakable foundation. It's the surest foundation you will ever have!

Lord, my life is in Your hands, period. Only what You say matters. I pray that Your perfect plan will be accomplished in my life. May I allow no other opinion to rival Yours. Thank You for Paul's stand recorded in Galatians 1:15-16 that encourages my very own stand and faithfulness to Your call. In Jesus' name, Amen.

Just for me in *Galatians*

56

Be with Us

2 Thessalonians 3:3, 16, "*But the Lord is faithful, and He will strengthen you and protect you from the evil one. . . . Now may the Lord of peace Himself give you peace at all times and in every way. The Lord be with all of you.*"

Nestled in this text is both a promise and a prayer for strength, protection, and peace. What emerges upon a slower, more intentional read is that all of this comes packaged in the Lord Himself. So, to frontload the point here, every prayer that the "Lord be with" anyone is a profound prayer.

Now, let me back up and admit that this prayer seems so simple, *too* simple. Sometimes, when this simple prayer is all that comes to mind, I rack my brain trying to think of a more profound, meaningful, specific, or descriptive way to pray. Surely there is a better way to pray *please be with the sick, please be with my family, please be with my friends, please be with the hurting, please be with the jobless, please be with* _____ (you fill in the blank). However, in 1 Thessalonians 3:3, 16, I am reintroduced to the true depth of that prayer.

In that simple request, "Lord be with them," we call on the presence of a faithful God, a dependable God, and a consistent God. We call on a powerful God who provides both the strength to handle the challenges that come, and also the protection from challenges that would come if the enemy had his way, unrestrained. We call on a God who is in full possession of peace, "the Lord of peace Himself." He has no shortage. He is able to supply peace "at all times and in every way." Don't we *all* need that? He is more than able to keep us in perfect peace, but we must trust Him completely (Isaiah 26:3, 12).

So I pray, reminded and reassured of the power in this simple prayer. Lord, be with us. Thank You for the power, protection, and peace in Your presence. There's no better place than with You. I'm so grateful, God. I bless Your name. Amen.

Just for me in 2 Thessalonians

57

More Than Just Talk

Malachi 3:16, "*Then those who feared the Lord talked with each other, and the Lord listened and heard. A scroll of remembrance was written in His presence concerning those who feared the Lord and honored His name.*"

Have you ever considered the possibility that conversations could be counted as prayer? Imagine this. You and your friends are relaxing. Not doing much. Just talking. In that moment, God tunes in. He captures your words and listens to the abundance of your heart as it flows from your lips.

Does this excite or mortify you?

I must say, this excites and motivates me to have uplifting, God-honoring conversations. It's such an opportunity to make a massive impact by letting every word count. It adds an intriguing nuance to the idea of continuous prayer. We must speak at all times with the confidence and awareness that God is listening, and He hears. Let's mind our mouths and make our words matter.

Lord, I am encouraged to have conversations worthy of Your remembrance. I pray that the words of my mouth and the meditations of my heart will be acceptable in Your sight (Psalm 19:14). I pray that my conversations will capture Your attention, and that my name will be a fixture on Your scroll. Amen.

Just for me in *Malachi*

58

Endless Praise

Revelation 7:9-12, *"After this I looked, and there before me was a great multitude that no one could count, from every nation, tribe, people and language, standing before the throne and before the Lamb. They were wearing white robes and were holding palm branches in their hands. And they cried out in a loud voice: 'Salvation belongs to our God, who sits on the throne, and to the Lamb.' All the angels were standing around the throne and around the elders and the four living creatures. They fell down on their faces before the throne and worshiped God, saying: 'Amen! Praise and glory and wisdom and thanks and honor and power and strength be to our God for ever and ever. Amen!'"*

This scene is larger than life. The throne of God is center stage, fully encircled with worshipers. There are those who are new to this experience, but who have no shortage of praise. There are the angels, elders, and creatures who are longtime residents in the very presence of God. This, however, does not alter their praise! The atmosphere is saturated with worship that is full, gushing, and unreservedly expressive.

I just love the expressions of praise recorded here! Excuse me while I borrow these words for a little practice of my own. In fact, *join me!* Here it goes: "Salvation belongs to our God, who sits on the throne, and to the Lamb. . . . Amen!" *(Deep breath!)* "Praise and glory and wisdom and thanks and honor and power and strength be to our God for ever and ever. Amen!"

God, I want to praise you like that! Even now, Lord, may praise flow freely from my lips directly to Your heart. With my entire being, I praise You. Let this be my lifestyle from now until eternity. This I pray with all sincerity. Amen.

Just for me in *Revelation*

59

Let Love Lead

2 John 1:6, "And this is love: that we walk in obedience to His commands. As you have heard from the beginning, His command is that you walk in love."

Walk in obedience. Walk in love. These two ideas are more than mutually informing. They are, in fact, one and the same. Our response to God's leadership is a direct reflection of our love for Him and, by extension, for others.

Let's briefly consider what is meant by walking in obedience to God's commands. While the "shall nots" and such of Exodus 20 most immediately come to mind, I've come to embrace that God's commands encompass so much more. They are both universal and personal.

The Ten Commandments, as well as other Biblical mandates, are universal. They are God-given commands to be upheld by everyone. No exceptions. Beyond this, however, it is also true that God makes specific asks of us as individuals. These are personal. He'll use our gifts, our spheres of influence, our personalities, our insecurities, and our experiences.

He may ask me to rise up an hour earlier to spend time with Him, but He may urge you to give financial gifts to families in need. He may impress you to listen rather than speak in a given situation. He may ask you to take on an unlikely client. These are also God's commands, His personal instructions just for you.

With every *yes* to God's commands, the universal and the personal, we will find that our path is sweetened by the fragrance of His matchless love. We will learn that walking in step with God truly is walking in love.

Lord, please strengthen my resolve to walk in step with every one of Your commands. I am asking that Your love fill the atmosphere of my heart, and may I remain in alignment with You. In my life, please be glorified. In Jesus' name I pray, Amen.

Just for me in **2 John**

60

Forever in Your Will

1 John 2:17, "The world and its desires pass away, but whoever does the will of God lives forever."

The world has some very attractive things to offer. I'm talking about appealing, exciting, alluring, tantalizing, and thrilling attractions. These things can cause us to daydream, to strive, to envy, and to grind. Somewhere deep in the fine print, however, is a terse one-liner.

The glittering is temporary, and all that glitters is not gold.

I wonder how different our responses to worldly attractions would be if they came plainly labeled with a "satisfaction expiration date." Would we reconsider engaging in them if these attractions came boldly stamped with just how far they would remove our hearts from God? I suspect the attraction factor would take a rapid nosedive.

1 John 2:17 tells us, "The world and its desires pass away, but whoever does the will of God lives forever." It is clear. The best option for now and eternity is to choose to do the will of God. Let His heart inform our desires. There is no expiration on the overflow of His goodness and love. That lifestyle will carry over seamlessly into eternity.

There is truly nothing worth more than life eternal with You, Lord. Anything else is temporary and at some point, tragically unsatisfying. Your will stretches into eternity, and it's Your will that I should live with You forever. That is exactly where I want to be. Help me not to stake my claim anywhere else or settle for anything else. Keep me forever in Your will. Amen.

Just for me in **1 John**

61

I'll Cry Out for Me

1 Chronicles 4:10, "Jabez cried out to the God of Israel, 'Oh, that You would bless me and enlarge my territory! Let Your hand be with me, and keep me from harm so that I will be free from pain.' And God granted his request."

There are times when I have felt utterly "unrighteous" and shamefully self-serving in my prayer life. In the middle of putting all of my desires, my hopes, my dreams, my needs, my frustrations (my, my, my, my . . .) on the table before God, a familiar feeling would guilt me into changing the subject. "Maybe I should turn that down a few notches, and instead, spend the time lifting up the needs of others. Surely, in the eyes of God, laboring in intercession rather than focusing the lens on myself is the right and pleasing thing to do."

Interceding for others is pleasing to God (1 Timothy 2:1, 3). However, this brief slice of Jabez's story in 1 Chronicles 4 lets us know that offering up a heartfelt prayer for ourselves is not distasteful to God.

Unashamedly, Jabez cried out on his own behalf. We don't know if he was suffering in physical or emotional pain, felt trapped by his perceived destiny, or struggled with the stigma attached to his name (it is suggested that his name sounds like the Hebrew word for pain). What we do know is Jabez could have lived the rest of his days with a sub-par existence: limited territory, harmful situations, and consistent pain. However, he saw a future free of all this only by the blessing and guidance of an eternally loving God. God heard his passionate cry and granted his request.

So, we don't need to flinch at the thought of pouring out our desires, our needs, our hopes, or even our frustrations. We can come to Him with all of our passion and with the very deepest parts of our hearts. I am reassured and I find great peace knowing that God hears every prayer, even the ones we pray for ourselves.

Lord, thank You for this truth. Help me to become far more comfortable and far less reserved in authentically expressing every part of myself to You. You know all; yet, You wait patiently to hear what's on my heart. Thank You for every answer You provide which is always what's best for me. In Jesus' name, I entrust myself to You fully. Amen.

Just for me in **1 Chronicles**

62

Live-Out-Loud Faith

Philemon 1:22, *"And one thing more: Prepare a guest room for me, because I hope to be restored to you in answer to your prayers."*

Throughout my lifetime, I have prayed an outlandish prayer or two. I remember well. My heart pulsed with desire and the belief that God can do anything. My prayers were saturated with petitions and pleas. Yet, I have found myself, more often than I wish to admit, holding expectation close to my chest. I was perfectly fine with testifying after God came through, but there was little chance of me allowing others to enter the vulnerable space of anticipation before He came through. I mean, what if God didn't respond? Wouldn't that look like God is incapable? Wouldn't *I* look a little crazy?

Can you see the cloaked pride peeking through?

Too often, we say we believe in God, but we shrink back from truly living out our faith. Silently, we whisper prayers. We hold our desires close. We play down our faith for fear of being disappointed.

Here, however, Paul models unabashed faith. From the dismal corner of a damp prison cell, He wraps up his letter to Philemon with a simple "by the way." Paul didn't just say, "Keep on praying for me." He confidently laid bare his expectation. "Prepare for my release. Get my room ready. You're praying. I'm believing." Paul expected God to move and he was unashamed to act like it and to ask others to do the same.

The reality is, self-protection and pride threaten and often cripple our faith walk. I receive Paul's simple request to Philemon as a reminder and an invitation to exhibit unreserved, active, live-out-loud faith. How about you?

Lord, I want to live my faith in all circumstances. Help me to be bold, and not shy or reserved about my expectation that You will come through. Speak to my heart. Make me sensitive to what would honor You in my living, even as I seek to live by faith. Forgive me for being prideful, when living my faith out loud could reach the hearts of others who need to be encouraged in their faith walk. I thank You even now for the active faith that will grow stronger in me from this day forward. Speak, Lord. Move in me. Take over. May I always remember it's never for me alone. I love You! Amen.

Just for me in *Philemon*

63

The Assurance of Victory

2 Chronicles 13:14-15, 18, *"Judah turned and saw that they were being attacked at both front and rear. Then they cried out to the Lord. The priests blew their trumpets and the men of Judah raised the battle cry. At the sound of their battle cry, God routed Jeroboam and all Israel before Abijah and Judah. . . . The Israelites were subdued on that occasion, and the people of Judah were victorious because they relied on the Lord, the God of their ancestors."*

At one time or another we've all felt overwhelmed and bombarded by life. Are you feeling that way right now? My simple encouragement is this: don't give up; look up! God is not intimidated by our circumstances, no matter how complex. Neither should we be.

Attacked on both sides? It didn't matter. The warriors of Judah knew exactly where their strength resided. They knew precisely from Whom their help came. It wasn't looking good for them, but in the heat of the conflict "they cried out to the Lord" and pressed on in battle. Moved by their faith, excited by their works, God was called to attention.

God, who never runs out of options.

God, who is never caught by surprise.

This God stood ready to move on their behalf.

The same God is our God. He is just as prepared to move on our behalf today. Judah experienced victory that day. In our most difficult seasons, we can have the assurance of victory too. Let it be our cry that gets God's attention. Nothing at all is too hard for Him, and let me add that nothing is too easy or unworthy of His notice. Call on Him for whatever presses on your heart. Cry out to God. Rely on God. He is good. He is powerful. He will act!

Thank You, Lord, for this reminder that trouble on every side is in no way intimidating to You. Even when it looks like we will lose and completely fail, You always win. Keep this truth always on my mind. With You, I will be victorious. Every. Single. Time. Amen.

Just for me in 2 Chronicles

64

A Promise of Better

Zechariah 1:17, *"Proclaim further: This is what the Lord Almighty says: 'My towns will again overflow with prosperity, and the Lord will again comfort Zion and choose Jerusalem.'"*

Have you ever been in a "dry" situation for too long? It's the kind of situation in which you deeply desire to experience change, but it stretches on day-after-day, year-after-year. It's a place where you feel sure that God put you; yet, it has become difficult to see the beauty in it and there's little to no thrill in it. Your prayer is for a change, an exciting change that pumps life back into your day and puts pep back into your step.

The proclamation in this text provides a window of hope.

Our situation can be revived; joy and prosperity can be restored. God has worked in this way before, and He can more than do it again.

Before we get to what God says in this verse, His words are contextualized. Zechariah 1:12-13 says the Lord spoke "kind and comforting words" in response to a question about the timing and experience of Judah's captive situation. What He promised in reply (v. 17) was not a basic reinstatement. It was the promise of abundant prosperity and His very presence. This is reminiscent of Jeremiah 29:11, where God declared that He had plans, a hope, and a prosperous future in store for His people.

When our present dismal, uncomfortable, frustrating season is all we see and feel, praise God He is still in control. If we remain in His hands, in due time, we will experience the overflowing prosperity that is in His ultimate plan.

What a good God You are! You don't desire to leave me lingering in a dry, unfulfilling place. The words of this verse were kind and comforting then, and they still are today. I'm so grateful to know that You can turn any situation into the very essence of an abundant life. Thank You for Your heart for my prosperity. I want to experience and enjoy every good and perfect plan You have for me. My heart is open for You to come in, to do any and all repair work, and to position me for prosperity. Thank You, Lord. Amen.

Just for me in *Zechariah*

65

Don't Shrink Back!

2 Timothy 1:6-7, "For this reason I remind you to fan into flame the gift of God, which is in you through the laying on of my hands. For the Spirit God gave us does not make us timid, but gives us power, love and self-discipline."

"Fan into flame the gift of God." This is a very intentional act. It is recognizing the gifts God has given and actively doing our part to grow them, not shrinking back and tucking them away.

"For the Spirit God gave us does not make us timid." Not only does this express God's desire that we not minimize our gifts, but it tells us that He empowers us to pursue the expansion of our gifts. He gives us all the "power, love, and self-discipline" we need to do this in a God-honoring manner.

To be honest, this verse could not have come at a better time for me. As I neared the end of this devotional experience, doubt crept in. "Should I really believe that my reflections matter or are profound enough to engage as a devotional resource? What if this comes across as shallow or juvenile? What if I share this with the world only to be rejected with eye-rolling critiques or missed expectations?"

My flame was dimming and was at risk of burning out, but God knew months ago that I would need this verse right now. This was a much-needed reminder that God did not place timidity in me. He gave me encouragement from His Word to fan into flame the gifts He has given. *He* accompanies those gifts with love, power, and "a sound mind" (KJV).

I receive this message and offer the same encouragement to you. Don't back off! Intentionally place yourself and every one of your gifts in God's hands to enlarge them and take them further than you thought could ever be.

The sincere payer of my heart is that You would be glorified in my life, Lord. I commit every ounce of my being to You. Show me just how to enlarge my gifts for Your glory. Show me how to live undaunted. May power, love, and self-discipline show up in everything I do. I pray that lives would be transformed in the process and at the end it can be said that my living was not in vain. I eagerly await that final affirmation from Your lips alone: "Well done." Until then, keep me faithful. In Jesus' name, I pray with all my heart, Amen.

Just for me in **2 Timothy**

66

It's Already Done

Titus 3:4-7, *"But when the kindness and love of God our Savior appeared, He saved us, not because of righteous things we had done, but because of His mercy. He saved us through the washing of rebirth and renewal by the Holy Spirit, whom He poured out on us generously through Jesus Christ our Savior, so that, having been justified by His grace, we might become heirs having the hope of eternal life."*

At the end of it all, it's all about God. Our very existence thrives on who He is and how He loves us so deeply, and so *generously*. He is our only reason for being. He is our only hope for eternity.

We occasionally find ourselves, however, running down the righteousness by works checklist as if there is anything we can do to merit salvation. Habitually, perhaps subconsciously, we take inventory and careful accounting of our time studying God's Word, interceding in prayer, preaching, teaching, performing acts of kindness, giving to charity, witnessing to a stranger, and anything else that ticks our well-intentioned yet woefully inconsequential "deserving Christian" scorecard.

No matter how many times or how many ways we run the calculations to prove our worthiness, our self-assessment comes up short.

It always does. It always will.

Praise God, salvation is not our responsibility. "He saved us," *(yes, it's already done)* "not because of righteous things we had done, but because of His mercy."

No expression of our kindness, no expansion of our gifts, none of our efforts to honor and please God are necessary for Him to pour out His kindness, love, mercy, grace, and saving power upon us. He receives us as we are. He loves us as we are. He transforms us through the Holy Spirit into who He created us to be. Let's rest in the saving grace of Jesus. He is all we will ever need, and He is enough.

God, it's all about You. My greatest, most sincere desire is life eternal with You. Help me to remember that You have already done the heavy lifting. It is not my place to strive and struggle, but to rest in You. Help me to walk out my faith with this assurance. Thank You for the hope of eternal life. I am eager to experience that new reality for which You paid dearly to offer me freely. By Your abundant mercy and immeasurable grace, I will be there. Amen.

Just for me in titus

Conclusion

Boundlessly Expectant

From cover to cover, we have found in God's Word life lessons, food for thought, smiles, laughs, peace, joy, new mantras, promises, reassurances, revelations, confirmation, motivation, inspiration, transformation, direction, clear views of God's heart, a deeper connection to Him, and so much more. My cup is running over!

It really is true. God does amazing things that we don't even expect (Isaiah 64:3). What I have learned from this experience and countless others is this: God makes it His business to shatter the glass ceilings of our expectations. He outdoes every imagination! He goes far beyond what we ask, think, or imagine. *He* is amazing!

I entered this experience expecting to build a habit of learning scripture. On the strength of His Word, I am exiting with greater expectations of an ever-deepening relationship with God. I am exiting with greater confidence that I can be, I *should* be, boundless in my expectations of Him. I am exiting with a personal experience that He truly takes little, and He makes it much! And yes, I am rolling out with sixty-six scriptures treasured in my heart!

I pray that your *Expectant* experience has opened you up to the realization that God is poised to minister to your heart from the expected and unexpected portions of His Word *and* your life. With renewed certainty, I can affirm the Bible is a gift, and all throughout, there is something just for you.

Let's continue to journey with God, expectantly, and see what amazing thing He does next!

Acknowledgments

To God, my loving heavenly Father – I owe it all to You! Thank You for every desire You have placed in my heart, especially every longing for You. I live to honor You!

To Rich, my wonderful husband, thank you for your tireless support: for reading, re-reading, listening, encouraging, and serving as the enduring hype-man! Thank you for allowing the Holy Spirit to lead in your life at home and at church, which is so central to how this journey unfolded. Thank you for trailblazing this book publishing path for our family. Let's keep striving to glorify God and to uplift humanity together. I love you!

To "Mothe," my dearest mommy, your love, support, and

example have been consistent throughout my entire life. My words are truly insufficient to articulate the depth of your God-honoring influence. For every bit of feedback that strengthened this project and simply for who you are, thank you! You are absolutely the real MVP. I love you like life!

To Nicole and Tanya, editors par excellence, thank you for using your God-given gifts to enhance this book in so many ways, tying up the loose ends and polishing off the rough edges. You have added to my many reasons to "Pause for Praise!"

To Brandon Taylor of Seek and Save Design, thank you for skillfully, patiently, and prayerfully bringing this vision to life! You have been a blessing.

To the numerous family, friends, and supporters who prayed, encouraged (knowingly or unknowingly), shared thoughts, utilized your voice, gifts, and resources for the success of this book, THANK YOU!

Notes

Day 12: *Well-Equipped by God to Please God | Hebrews 13:20-21*

[1] Ellen G. White, "Growing Up Into Christ," in Steps to Christ, (Hagerstown, MD: Foy Institute Press, 1995). 71-72.

Day 39: *Every Single Thing | Genesis 6:22*

[2] Ellen G. White, "The Gift of the Spirit," in Acts of the Apostles, (Portland, OR: Pacific Press Publishing Association, 1911). 51.

In Order of Biblical Appearance

Other Resources

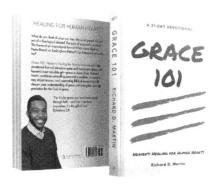

Grace 101: Heaven's Healing for Human Hearts is a 31-day devotional that will introduce some and reacquaint others with heaven's most valuable gift—grace in Jesus Christ. Richard Martin combines compelling personal anecdotes, contemporary object lessons, and captivating Biblical stories that will deepen your understanding of grace and strengthen your appreciation for the God of grace.

Available at www.richdmartin.com.

Ordered Steps: A Guide to Knowing God's Will for Your Life

You and I have something in common. We both want to know God's will for our lives. We are not alone either. We share the company of thousands, even millions, who also desire to live their lives squarely in the will of God. You may be wondering, "Can I really know God's will for my life?" You can, and the prayer of this resource is that you will. As you embark on this journey, I pray that you come to know God better than you do right now. For, seeking God's will ultimately begins and ends with seeking God.

Available at www.richdmartin.com.

About the Author

Kylah R. S. Martin (née Allers) was born and raised in the paradise island of Bermuda. She is a loyal, lively, fun-loving friend who sees beauty in connecting with others and, most importantly, with God. Her compassionate spirit and servant's heart fuel her desire to help others experience new depths with Jesus Christ – be they man, woman, boy, or girl. Kylah values spending quality time with family and friends, solving interesting problems, cultivating and refining ideas, traveling to scenic destinations, sharing meaningful experiences with just about anyone, and laughing to tears. She holds a BBA in Health Care Administration from Oakwood University, an MS in Community and International Development from Andrews University, and a Professional in Human Resources certification from HRCI. Kylah and the love of her life, Richard, have made it their shared commitment to glorify God and uplift others.

Stay connected with Kylah and others from the *Expectant* devotional community.

Website: www.iexpectGod.com

Instagram: @iexpect_God

Made in United States
Orlando, FL
27 December 2022